You are about to read the coolest History series ever written.

"Make History Wavy again"

THE KINGDOM OF ISRAEL

The Ancient Kingdom that Played a Key Role in Biblical History

The Kingdom of Israel

The Kingdom of Israel

Copyright © 2024 What The History

No part of this publication may be reproduced, stored in a retrieval system, or transmitted in any form or by any means, electronic, mechanical, photocopying, recording, or otherwise, without the prior written permission of the publisher.

Printed in the United States of America

First Edition: 2024

This copyright page includes the necessary copyright notice, permissions request information, acknowledgments for the cover design, interior design, and editing, as well as the details of the first edition.

www.littlebiggiant.com

Disclaimer: This book is a work of non-fiction and is intended for informational and educational purposes only. The names in this biography are trademarks of their respective owners. This book is not affiliated with, endorsed by, or sponsored by any of these trademark holders. The use of these names is intended solely to provide context and historical reference.

The author makes no claims to ownership of any trademarks or copyrights associated with the names and likenesses of the individuals referenced in this book. Any opinions expressed in this book are those of the author and do not reflect the views of any wrestling promotion or trademark holder.

Introduction

Once upon a time, in the land of ancient Israel, there was this super cool kingdom that was like, totally important in the Bible. Picture this: around 1000 BCE, a dude named King David came along and united all the tribes. It was like the ultimate squad goals! He made Jerusalem the capital, and it was lit! But wait, it gets even crazier. His son, Solomon, built this epic temple that was like the biggest flex ever. People from all over came to check it out, and it was a total game-changer for the region.

But then, things got a bit messy. After Solomon kicked the bucket, the kingdom split into two—Israel in the north and Judah in the south. Talk about drama! This split led to all sorts of wild events, like battles, prophets, and even some serious betrayals. The stories from this time are packed with action, mystery, and lessons that still matter today. So, what really went down in this ancient kingdom? Buckle up, because the adventure is just getting started!

Table of Contents

Table of Contents.. 8
Chapter 1...11
The Birth of a Nation - Discover how the Kingdom of Israel began with a promise and a journey.............. 11
Chapter 2...19
The Mighty Kings... 19
Chapter 3...28
The Heart of Worship... 28
Chapter 4...38
The Prophets' Voice.. 38
Chapter 5...46
Epic Battles and Heroes..46
Chapter 6...55
Daily Life in Ancient Israel.......................................55
Chapter 7...63
The Land of Milk and Honey................................... 63
Chapter 8...72
The Art of Storytelling..72

Chapter 9 .... **82**
The Legacy of Israel 82
Chapter 10 .... **91**
Mysteries and Myths 91

The Kingdom of Israel

Chapter 1

The Birth of a Nation - Discover how the Kingdom of Israel began with a promise and a journey.

Once upon a time, in a land far away, there was a man named Abraham. He was a kind and curious man who loved to explore the world around him. One day, while sitting under the shade of a great tree, he heard a voice that changed everything. This voice was from God, who made a special promise to Abraham. "I will make you the father of a great nation," God said. "Your descendants will be as numerous as the stars in the sky!"

Imagine standing under a vast night sky, where twinkling stars stretch as far as your eyes can see. Each star represents a family, a story, and a journey. Abraham felt a spark of excitement in his heart. He knew that this promise meant he would be part of something much bigger than himself.

But there was one little problem: Abraham and his wife, Sarah, were very old and had no children. They faced many challenges on their journey, but they believed in the promise. They packed their belongings and set off on an adventure, traveling to a new land called Canaan. This land was like a treasure waiting to be discovered, filled with lush green hills, sparkling rivers, and golden fields. It was a place where they could grow and thrive.

As they traveled, they met many people and faced many hardships. There were times when they felt lost and afraid, but Abraham held onto his faith like a bright lantern in the dark. He taught his family to trust in the promise, to be brave, and to keep moving forward, no matter what. His journey wasn't just about finding a new home; it was about building a new life.

Years passed, and miraculously, Sarah gave birth to a son named Isaac. It was as if the stars had finally aligned! Isaac was the first of many descendants, and the promise began to blossom like a beautiful flower. Abraham's family grew, and soon there were more and more people who believed in the same promise. They were united by faith and hope, creating bonds that were stronger than any rope.

As time went on, Isaac had a son named Jacob, who later became known as Israel. Jacob had twelve sons, and these sons became the leaders of the twelve tribes of Israel. Picture a colorful tapestry woven with different threads, each thread representing a tribe with its own unique story. Together, they formed a community that would grow and flourish.

The journey of the Kingdom of Israel was not just about land; it was about the spirit of a people who believed in a promise. It was about families coming together, sharing stories around the fire, and dreaming of a bright future. They faced many challenges, including hunger, battles, and even slavery, but through it all, they held onto their identity and faith.

As the sun set on the horizon, painting the sky in hues of orange and purple, the people of Israel gathered to celebrate their heritage. They sang songs of hope and resilience, remembering the journey that brought them together. It was a beautiful reminder that even in the toughest times, they were never alone.

The birth of the Kingdom of Israel teaches us that promises can lead to great things, and that even the smallest journey can create a mighty nation. It shows us the importance of faith, family, and the courage to keep moving forward, no matter how difficult the path may seem.

Key Takeaway: Just like Abraham, we can hold onto our dreams and promises, believing that even the smallest beginnings can lead to something great.

Chapter 2

The Mighty Kings

In the ancient land of Israel, where the sun kissed the earth and the stars whispered secrets to the night, there lived a series of mighty kings who shaped the destiny of a nation. Imagine a time when the world was young, and the air was filled with the sounds of laughter, the rustling of leaves, and the distant calls of shepherds tending their flocks.

This is the story of Israel's greatest kings, from the humble beginnings of Saul to the wise reign of Solomon.

Let's start with King Saul, the first king of Israel. Picture a tall man with broad shoulders and a heart full of dreams. He was chosen by the people to lead them, a brave warrior who fought against the enemies of Israel. But Saul's story wasn't just about battles and victories; it was also about the struggles within himself. He often felt unsure and worried, like a ship lost at sea. Imagine standing on a cliff, looking out at the vast ocean, feeling the waves crash against the rocks below. That was how Saul felt when he faced the challenges of being a king. His journey teaches us that even the mightiest can feel fear, but it's how we face that fear that truly matters.

Next came King David, a shepherd boy who became a legendary king. Can you picture him sitting under a tree, strumming his harp, singing songs that echoed through the hills? David was not just a warrior; he was an artist, a poet, and a dreamer. He faced a giant named Goliath, a fearsome opponent that made everyone else tremble. With nothing but a sling and a stone, David stepped forward, his heart pounding like a drum. He believed in himself and his God, and with a single throw, he defeated Goliath. This moment wasn't just about winning a battle; it was about believing in the impossible. David's courage reminds us that no matter how small we may feel, we can achieve great things if we have faith in ourselves.

As David ruled, he united the tribes of Israel and made Jerusalem the capital. Imagine a bustling city filled with merchants, musicians, and families celebrating together. David danced with joy, bringing the Ark of the Covenant to Jerusalem, a symbol of God's presence among the people. His reign was filled with love and music, but it wasn't without challenges. David faced betrayal and loss, teaching us that even the greatest leaders have to overcome heartache. His story encourages us to embrace our emotions and to find strength in our vulnerability.

Then came King Solomon, David's son, known for his wisdom. Picture a wise old owl perched on a branch, observing the world with keen eyes. Solomon was famous for his ability to solve problems and make fair decisions. One day, two women came to him, each claiming to be the mother of a baby. Solomon, with his clever mind, proposed to cut the baby in half so each woman could have a piece. The real mother immediately cried out, willing to give up her claim to save her child. Solomon recognized her love and gave her the baby, teaching everyone that true wisdom lies in understanding the hearts of others. Solomon's story reminds us to listen and empathize with those around us, for wisdom is not just about knowing facts but also about understanding feelings.

As we explore the lives of these kings, we see a tapestry woven with bravery, love, wisdom, and challenges. Each king faced trials that tested their strength and character, and their stories resonate with us today. They remind us that being a leader is not just about wearing a crown or sitting on a throne; it's about making choices that affect others, showing kindness, and learning from our mistakes.

Why do we look back at these kings? Because their stories are not just tales of the past; they are lessons for our future. They inspire us to be brave like David, wise like Solomon, and to face our fears like Saul. As we navigate our own lives, we can carry their lessons in our hearts, remembering that we too can be mighty in our own way.

Key Takeaway: The stories of Israel's kings teach us that courage, wisdom, and empathy are powerful traits that can help us overcome challenges and make a positive impact on the world around us.

The Kingdom of Israel

Chapter 3

The Heart of Worship

In the ancient Kingdom of Israel, nestled among the rolling hills and golden fields, stood a magnificent structure that was the heart of worship for the Israelites—the Temple. Imagine a place so grand that its beauty sparkled like the stars in the night sky. The Temple was not just a building; it was a sacred space where the people connected with God, a place filled with prayers, songs, and the sweet aroma of offerings.

The Temple was built in Jerusalem, a city that shone like a jewel, with its towering walls and bustling streets. King Solomon, the wise ruler of Israel, was the one who built this magnificent Temple around 957 BCE. He wanted to create a home for the Ark of the Covenant, which held the sacred tablets of the Ten Commandments. Picture the Ark as a treasure chest filled with the most important rules given to the Israelites, guiding them on how to live good and loving lives.

As the sun rose each day, casting a golden glow over the Temple, the Israelites would gather in anticipation. They came from far and wide, traveling through valleys and over hills, their hearts filled with hope and reverence. The Temple was a place where they could express their gratitude to God, ask for forgiveness, and seek guidance. It was like a giant hug from the heavens, reminding them that they were never alone.

Inside the Temple, the air was thick with the sound of prayers rising like incense. Imagine the flickering candles illuminating the faces of worshippers, their eyes shining with faith. The priests, dressed in beautiful robes, led the ceremonies with a sense of purpose and grace. They would offer sacrifices—like lambs and doves—symbolizing the people's devotion and love for God. These acts were not just rituals; they were heartfelt expressions of their hopes and dreams.

But the Temple was more than just a place of sacrifice; it was a center of community.

Families would come together, sharing stories and laughter, creating bonds that would last a lifetime. It was a space where people felt connected, not just to each other, but to something much greater than themselves. As they sang songs of praise, their voices blended together like a beautiful symphony, echoing through the stone walls, reaching the heavens above.

Yet, the story of the Temple is not just one of beauty and devotion. It is also a tale of loss and resilience. Over the years, the Temple faced many challenges. It was destroyed and rebuilt, but each time it rose from the ashes like a phoenix, reminding the Israelites of their strength and faith. They learned that even in the darkest times, their connection to God and to each other could never be broken.

The Temple also served as a reminder of the importance of worship in their daily lives. It taught the Israelites that worship was not just something they did on special occasions; it was a way of life. Every act of kindness, every moment of gratitude, and every prayer whispered in the quiet of the night was a form of worship. They learned that God was always listening, always present, even when they were far from the Temple.

As we ponder the significance of the Temple in the lives of the Israelites, we are invited to reflect on our own lives. What does it mean to worship? How do we connect with the world around us and with something greater than ourselves? The Temple reminds us that worship can take many forms, whether it's through acts of kindness, moments of reflection, or simply being present for one another.

In this vast universe, where stars twinkle like tiny candles, we are all part of a cosmic story. Just as the Israelites found their heart of worship in the Temple, we too can find our own places of connection and love, whether in nature, in our communities, or within ourselves.

Key Takeaway: Worship is not just a place we go; it's a way of living that connects us to each other and to something greater. Just like the Israelites found their heart of worship in the Temple, we can discover our own special ways to express love, gratitude, and kindness every day.

The Kingdom of Israel

CHAPTER 4

The Prophets' Voice

In the ancient Kingdom of Israel, a land filled with rolling hills, shimmering rivers, and bustling towns, there were brave men and women known as prophets. Imagine standing on a high hill, the sun setting in a blaze of orange and pink, casting a warm glow over the land. You hear the rustling of leaves and the distant sound of children laughing. But amidst this beauty, the people sometimes forgot to be kind and just. This is where the prophets stepped in, like shining stars in a dark night.

The prophets were special messengers chosen by God. They had a remarkable ability to see beyond the ordinary, to understand the world around them, and to speak the truth, even when it was hard to hear. One of the most famous prophets was a man named Isaiah. Picture him, a tall figure with a long beard, standing in the center of a crowded marketplace, his voice rising above the chatter. "Listen, people of Israel!" he would call out, his words echoing like thunder. "You must care for the poor and treat each other with love! If you do not, the world will become a dark place!"

Isaiah's words were like a gentle breeze that stirred the hearts of the people. He reminded them of their responsibility to each other, urging them to be just and fair. But not everyone wanted to listen. Sometimes, the kings and leaders of Israel became too powerful and greedy. They built grand palaces and forgot about the people who were suffering. The prophets, like brave knights in shining armor, stood up to these rulers. They faced danger and often spoke in riddles, using stories to teach important lessons.

Another prophet, Jeremiah, was known for his deep compassion. Imagine him walking through the streets, tears in his eyes, as he saw people turning away from goodness. "Why do you ignore the cries of the needy?" he would plead. His heart was heavy with the weight of their struggles. He was like a mother hen trying to gather her chicks under her wings, wanting to protect them from harm. Jeremiah's words were a call to action, reminding the people that they were all part of one family, and they needed to care for one another.

And then there was Elijah, a fiery prophet who challenged the false gods worshipped by some of the people. Picture him standing on a mountain, the wind whipping through his hair, as he called down fire from the sky to prove that the God of Israel was the true God. The people gasped in awe as flames danced before them, illuminating the night. Elijah's courage inspired many, and his story became legendary, reminding everyone that standing up for what is right can change the course of history.

The prophets' messages were not just about rules and laws; they were about love, justice, and compassion. They taught the people that every action mattered, like ripples in a pond. When someone helped a neighbor, it spread joy like sunshine breaking through the clouds. But when they turned away from kindness, it created shadows that lingered.

As you read about these brave prophets, you might wonder: What would it be like to stand up for what is right? How can we be like them in our own lives? The prophets' voices remind us that we all have a part to play in making the world a better place. They challenge us to think about our actions and how they affect those around us.

So, the next time you see someone in need or witness an unfair situation, remember the prophets of Israel. Be brave like Isaiah, compassionate like Jeremiah, and courageous like Elijah. You have the power to make a difference, just like they did.

Key Takeaway: The prophets of Israel teach us the importance of speaking up for what is right and caring for one another. Just like them, we can be brave and compassionate in our everyday lives, making the world a better place for everyone.

Chapter 5

Epic Battles and Heroes

In the heart of ancient Israel, where the sun cast golden rays over rolling hills and olive groves, the air was often filled with the sounds of clashing swords and the battle cries of brave warriors. The Kingdom of Israel was not just a place of peace and worship; it was a land where epic battles unfolded, shaping the destiny of its people and leaving behind tales of heroism that still echo through time.

Imagine standing on a rocky hilltop, your heart pounding with excitement as you watch a great army gather below. This was the scene at the Valley of Elah, where the mighty warrior David faced off against the giant Goliath. Goliath was a fearsome Philistine, towering over everyone like a mountain, clad in heavy armor that glinted in the sunlight. The Israelites trembled in fear, but young David, a shepherd boy with a heart full of courage, stepped forward. With nothing but a slingshot and five smooth stones, he believed he could defeat the giant.

As the tension built, David's voice rang out, "You come against me with sword and spear, but I come against you in the name of the Lord!" With a swift motion, he hurled a stone that struck Goliath right in the forehead, sending the giant crashing to the ground. The cheers of the Israelites erupted like fireworks in the sky, marking the beginning of David's journey from shepherd to king. This battle taught the people that true strength comes not from size or weapons, but from faith and bravery.

But the story of battles in Israel didn't end there. Fast forward to the reign of King Saul, where the Israelites faced the relentless threat of the Philistines once more. Picture a dark night, the moon casting shadows over the campfires of the Israelite army. King Saul, a tall and imposing figure, felt the weight of his people's hopes on his shoulders. He knew they had to fight to protect their land. With swords raised high, the Israelites charged into battle, their hearts beating as one, united against a common enemy.

One of the most famous battles during this time was the Battle of Michmash. The Israelites, outnumbered and outmatched, found themselves in a desperate situation. But then, a courageous young warrior named Jonathan, the son of King Saul, decided to take a bold step. He and his armor-bearer climbed a steep cliff, surprising the enemy with a sudden attack. Their bravery sparked a fire in the hearts of the Israelite soldiers, who rallied behind them, turning the tide of the battle. This moment showed everyone that even in the darkest times, a single act of courage can light the way to victory.

As the Kingdom of Israel continued to grow, so did the legends of its heroes. One such hero was Gideon, a man chosen by God to lead the Israelites against the Midianites. Gideon started with a small army, but he was determined to fight for his people. With clever tactics and unwavering faith, he devised a plan that involved torches and trumpets. When the Israelites surrounded the Midianite camp at night, they lit their torches and blew their trumpets, creating a noise so loud that the Midianites were thrown into confusion, believing they were being attacked by a massive army. They fled in fear, and Israel was saved! This battle reminded everyone that with cleverness and faith, even the smallest group can achieve great things.

As we explore these epic battles, it's important to remember that the heroes of Israel were not just warriors; they were also leaders, thinkers, and people of faith. Their stories teach us about the power of courage, the importance of unity, and the belief that anyone can be a hero, regardless of their size or background.

So, as you ponder these thrilling tales of bravery and valor, think about the lessons they hold. How can you be brave in your own life? What challenges do you face, and how can you face them with the same courage as David, Jonathan, and Gideon?

Key Takeaway: Courage comes in many forms. Whether you're facing a big challenge or standing up for what's right, remember that even the smallest act of bravery can make a huge difference. Be a hero in your own story!

Chapter 6

Daily Life in Ancient Israel

In the Kingdom of Israel, life was a tapestry woven with vibrant colors, sounds, and scents. Imagine waking up in a cozy mud-brick home, the sun peeking through a small window, casting warm rays across the straw mat where you slept. You can hear the gentle clucking of chickens and the distant sounds of sheep bleating in the fields. The air is fresh, filled with the earthy scent of the land after the morning dew.

As you stretch and yawn, the aroma of fresh bread baking fills the air. Your mother is in the kitchen, mixing flour and water to make dough. She shapes the bread into flat rounds, ready to be baked on the hot stones of the oven. "Breakfast is almost ready!" she calls, her voice bright and cheerful. You can hardly wait to taste the warm, fluffy bread, spread with a little honey or olive oil.

After breakfast, it's time to help with chores. If you're a boy, you might head out to the fields with your father, where the golden wheat sways gently in the breeze. You'll learn how to plant seeds, carefully placing them in the rich soil, or maybe you'll help with the harvest, cutting the tall stalks with a curved sickle. If you're a girl, you might help your mother gather water from the nearby well, the cool water splashing against your hands as you fill your clay jars.

But it's not all work! After the chores are done, there's time for play. You and your friends might gather in a sunny spot to play games like tag or hide-and-seek. The laughter echoes like music, and for a moment, you forget about the hard work that comes with living in ancient Israel. Sometimes, you might even gather around a storyteller, who spins tales of heroes and gods, their voices rising and falling like the waves of the sea.

As the sun begins to set, painting the sky with shades of orange and purple, your family gathers for dinner. You sit together on a woven mat, sharing stories about your day. The food is simple but delicious—perhaps lentil stew, fresh vegetables, and the bread your mother baked in the morning. It's a time to bond, to share laughter, and to feel grateful for the day's blessings.

In ancient Israel, the community was important. People worked together, celebrating festivals and special occasions as one big family. When harvest time came, everyone joined in, singing songs and dancing under the stars. The air was filled with joy and the sweet smell of ripe fruits and grains.

But life wasn't always easy. There were challenges, too. Sometimes, there were droughts, and the fields would dry up. People had to come together to find solutions, sharing what little food they had and helping each other through tough times. They learned the importance of kindness and cooperation, understanding that they were stronger together.

As night falls, the stars twinkle above like diamonds scattered across a dark velvet sky. You lie on your mat, looking up at the constellations. Each star seems to tell a story, connecting you to the world beyond. You might wonder about the lives of people far away, or what lies beyond the horizon.

Living in the Kingdom of Israel was like being part of a grand adventure, filled with work, laughter, and love. Each day brought new experiences, lessons, and memories that would last a lifetime.

Key Takeaway: Life in ancient Israel was a blend of hard work and joyful play, teaching us the importance of community, cooperation, and appreciating the simple moments we share with our families and friends.

Chapter 7

The Land of Milk and Honey

Once upon a time, in a land nestled between the Mediterranean Sea and the vast deserts, there was a place known as Israel. This enchanting land was often called the "Land of Milk and Honey," and it earned this name for many wonderful reasons. Imagine rolling hills, lush green valleys, and sparkling rivers that danced through the landscape like playful children. The beauty of Israel was not just in its sights but also in the treasures hidden within its soil.

Israel is a small country, but its geography is incredibly diverse. In the north, you would find the majestic mountains of Galilee, where the air is fresh and cool, and the scenery is dotted with beautiful flowers and trees. It's like stepping into a painter's masterpiece! As you travel south, the land transforms into golden deserts, where the sun shines brightly and the sand stretches endlessly, creating a warm embrace for those who wander through it.

One of the most remarkable features of Israel is the Jordan River. This river flows like a silver ribbon through the land, bringing life to everything around it. It's not just a river; it's a source of hope and nourishment for the people, animals, and plants that call this land home. Picture farmers tending to their fields, using the river's water to grow delicious fruits and vegetables, from juicy oranges to sweet pomegranates. This is how the land flourished, with nature providing all the ingredients for a bountiful life.

Now, let's talk about the natural resources that made Israel so special. The land was rich in minerals and fertile soil, which allowed farmers to cultivate crops that were not only abundant but also delicious. Wheat, barley, and grapes grew plentifully, and these crops were the backbone of the economy. Can you imagine biting into a warm, freshly baked loaf of bread made from wheat grown right there in the fields? Or sipping sweet grape juice from the fruits of the vine? It's a taste of heaven!

But the treasures of Israel didn't stop at crops. The Mediterranean Sea, with its shimmering blue waves, offered a bounty of fish and seafood. Fishermen would set out early in the morning, casting their nets into the sparkling waters, hoping to catch the day's meal. The sea was like a treasure chest, filled with wonders waiting to be discovered. The people of Israel learned to respect the ocean, taking only what they needed and giving thanks for the gifts it provided.

As we explore this magical land, we can't forget about the mountains and hills that surround it. These towering giants were not just beautiful; they were also rich in minerals like limestone and clay, which the people used to build their homes and create pottery. Imagine climbing a mountain and standing at the top, feeling the cool breeze on your face and looking out over the land that has so much history and life. It would be a breathtaking view, a reminder of the beauty and resources that surrounded them.

But why is this land called the "Land of Milk and Honey"? Well, milk comes from the sheep and goats that grazed on the lush pastures, while honey was harvested from the bees that buzzed happily among the flowers. Together, they symbolized abundance and sweetness, representing a life filled with nourishment and joy. It was a place where people could thrive, where the earth provided everything they needed to live well.

As we think about Israel and its natural wonders, we can ask ourselves some big questions. What does it mean to take care of the land we live on? How can we ensure that our resources are used wisely, just like the people of Israel did? And how can we appreciate the beauty around us, from the mountains to the rivers, and the plants and animals that share our home?

In the end, Israel was not just a place on a map; it was a living, breathing ecosystem, full of life and opportunity. The geography and natural resources made it unique and prosperous, a true treasure in the heart of the world.

Key Takeaway: The land we live on is full of resources that can help us thrive, but it's important to take care of it and use those resources wisely. Just like the people of Israel, we can learn to appreciate and protect the beauty around us!

Chapter 8

The Art of Storytelling

Once upon a time, in the sun-kissed lands of ancient Israel, where the golden sands met the shimmering blue of the Mediterranean Sea, there was a magical tradition that wove the fabric of their culture together:

storytelling. Imagine sitting around a crackling fire under a sky full of twinkling stars, the air filled with the sweet scent of roasted figs and the soft murmur of the night. This was a time when families gathered, and the elders shared tales that danced through the air like the flames before them.

In Israel, storytelling wasn't just a way to pass the time; it was a treasure chest filled with history, lessons, and dreams. The stories of the past were like precious gems, each one sparkling with the wisdom of generations. They told of brave kings and queens, of battles fought and won, and of the everyday lives of the people who called this land home. One of the most famous storytellers was a young shepherd boy named David. He would sit under the shade of olive trees, strumming his harp, and enchanting everyone with his songs about bravery and faith. His stories inspired the hearts of his people, reminding them of their strength and unity.

As the sun dipped below the horizon, casting a warm orange glow over the hills, the elders would share stories of the great King Solomon, known for his wisdom and fairness.

They spoke of how he built the magnificent Temple in Jerusalem, a place where people came to pray and seek guidance. "Did you know," an elder would say, leaning closer, "that Solomon once solved a dispute between two mothers fighting over a baby? He suggested to split the baby in two! But the true mother, filled with love, immediately offered to give up her claim to save her child. Solomon knew then who the real mother was!" The children's eyes would widen with awe, their imaginations ignited by the vivid images painted by the storyteller's words.

But storytelling wasn't just about the past; it was also a way to teach important lessons. Each tale carried a message, like a hidden treasure waiting to be discovered. The stories taught values like kindness, courage, and the importance of community. For instance, the tale of the Good Samaritan, a story about helping others regardless of differences, reminded everyone to show compassion to their neighbors. The lessons woven into these narratives were like seeds planted in the hearts of the listeners, growing into actions that shaped their lives.

As the years passed, the art of storytelling continued to thrive, even in the face of challenges. The people of Israel faced many trials, including invasions and exiles. But through it all, they held onto their stories like lifebuoys in a stormy sea. They gathered in secret, whispering tales of hope and resilience, ensuring that their history would never fade away. The stories became a bridge connecting the past with the present, allowing future generations to understand their roots and identity.

Imagine, if you will, a young girl named Miriam, who listened intently to her grandmother's tales. Each night, as she lay in bed, she would close her eyes and picture the heroes and heroines from the stories, feeling as if she were part of their adventures. She learned about the importance of faith and courage, and how the stories of her ancestors were like a compass, guiding her through life's challenges. Miriam dreamed of one day becoming a storyteller herself, sharing the rich tapestry of her people's history with the world.

Storytelling in Israel was not just a pastime; it was a lifeline. It preserved their culture and identity, even when faced with adversity. The stories became a shared experience, a way for families and communities to come together, reinforcing bonds that time could not break. The echoes of laughter, gasps of surprise, and even the tears shed during poignant moments filled the air, creating a symphony of emotions that united everyone around the fire.

As we reflect on this beautiful tradition, we can ask ourselves: How do our own stories shape who we are? What lessons do we carry from our own experiences? Just like the people of Israel, we too can weave our stories into the fabric of our lives, sharing them with others and learning from one another.

Key Takeaway: Storytelling is a powerful way to share history, teach important lessons, and connect with others. Our stories help shape our identity and bring people together, reminding us that we are all part of a larger tapestry of life.

The Kingdom of Israel

Chapter 9

The Legacy of Israel

In the heart of ancient times, nestled between rolling hills and shimmering rivers, the Kingdom of Israel blossomed like a radiant flower in the desert. Its people, rich in culture and wisdom, left a legacy that would ripple through time, touching the lives of countless generations around the globe. But how did this small kingdom, with its stories of kings, prophets, and battles, shape the world we know today?

Imagine a bustling marketplace in Jerusalem, where merchants shouted out their wares, and children laughed as they played in the sun-drenched streets. This vibrant city was not just a center of trade; it was a melting pot of ideas, beliefs, and traditions. The Kingdom of Israel was known for its groundbreaking contributions to religion, philosophy, and law. The stories of its kings, like David and Solomon, were filled with bravery and wisdom, teaching lessons about leadership and justice that still resonate today.

One of the most significant gifts the Kingdom of Israel gave to the world was the concept of monotheism—the belief in one God. This idea was revolutionary! Imagine living in a time when people worshipped many gods, each with their own stories and demands. The Israelites, however, believed in a single, all-powerful God who created the universe and cared for His people. This belief would go on to influence major religions like Judaism, Christianity, and Islam, shaping the spiritual lives of billions of people.

Think of the stories in the Bible, filled with adventure, moral lessons, and divine encounters. These tales, passed down through generations, taught values like kindness, justice, and the importance of community. They inspired great thinkers, artists, and leaders throughout history. For instance, during the Renaissance, artists like

Michelangelo and Leonardo da Vinci drew inspiration from biblical stories, creating masterpieces that still captivate us today.

But the legacy of Israel didn't stop at religion and art. The kingdom also laid the groundwork for laws that would influence societies around the world. The Ten Commandments, a set of moral guidelines given to Moses, became a cornerstone for many legal systems. Imagine a world where rules were not just about punishment but also about fairness and respect for one another. These ancient laws remind us that even in the midst of chaos, there is a call for order and compassion.

As we look beyond the borders of ancient Israel, we see how its ideas traveled far and wide. The Silk Road, a network of trade routes, connected different cultures, allowing the teachings and stories of Israel to spread like seeds carried by the wind. From the deserts of the Middle East to the bustling cities of Europe, the legacy of Israel found its way into the hearts and minds of people everywhere.

But what does this all mean for us today? Why should we care about a kingdom that existed thousands of years ago? Well, the legacy of Israel teaches us that our actions and beliefs can have a lasting impact. It invites us to think about how we treat one another and the values we uphold in our communities. Are we spreading kindness like seeds in a garden, or are we allowing negativity to take root?

As we ponder our place in this grand story, we might ask ourselves: How can we carry forward the lessons of justice, compassion, and unity that the Kingdom of Israel championed? In a world that often feels divided, we can strive to be bridges, connecting people through understanding and respect.

So, the next time you gaze up at the stars or listen to a story from the past, remember the Kingdom of Israel—a small kingdom with a mighty legacy that continues to inspire us all.

Key Takeaway: The Kingdom of Israel taught us the importance of belief, justice, and compassion, reminding us that our actions today can shape the world for future generations.

Chapter 10

Mysteries and Myths

In the ancient Kingdom of Israel, stories and legends flowed like the rivers that nourished the land. These tales were woven into the fabric of everyday life, much like the colorful tapestries that adorned the walls of homes. They spoke of heroes, miracles, and events that seemed to stretch the very limits of imagination. As we explore these mysteries and myths, we will embark on a journey that takes us through time, revealing the wonders and questions that have captivated hearts and minds for centuries.

Imagine walking through the bustling streets of Jerusalem, where merchants shout about their wares, and children play games in the dusty alleys. The air is filled with the sweet scent of freshly baked bread and the distant sound of music from a lyre. In this vibrant city, stories of King David, the shepherd boy who became a mighty warrior, echoed through the stone walls. But there was more to David than just his bravery; he was said to have danced before the Ark of the Covenant, a sacred chest that held the tablets of the Ten Commandments. The Ark was believed to be a direct connection to God, and its presence filled the people with awe.

One of the most fascinating legends surrounding the Kingdom of Israel is the story of the lost tribes. After King Solomon's reign, the kingdom split into two: Israel in the north and Judah in the south. The northern kingdom eventually fell to the Assyrians, and many of its people vanished from history, leading to the mystery of the ten lost tribes. Where did they go? Some believe they traveled far away, while others think they blended into other cultures. This enigma has sparked countless theories and fueled the imaginations of adventurers and historians alike.

Then there's the story of the miraculous walls of Jericho. According to the Bible, when the Israelites, led by Joshua, approached the city, they were faced with towering walls that seemed impenetrable. But with faith and a peculiar strategy—marching around the city for seven days and blowing trumpets—the walls crumbled to the ground. This tale of faith and perseverance teaches us that sometimes, even the most daunting challenges can be overcome with determination and belief.

As we delve deeper into the mysteries of the ancient Kingdom of Israel, we encounter the enigmatic figure of the prophet Elijah. Known for his fiery spirit and miraculous deeds, Elijah was said to have called down fire from the heavens to prove the power of God. His story is filled with drama and suspense, as he challenged the prophets of Baal to a contest. The tension in the air was palpable as the two sides prayed for their gods to send fire to consume their offerings. When Elijah's prayer was answered, and fire rained down, it was a moment of pure wonder that left the people in awe.

But not all mysteries are wrapped in tales of glory. The ancient Kingdom of Israel also faced dark times, such as the Babylonian exile, when the people were taken from their homeland and scattered like leaves in the wind. This event raised profound questions about identity and faith. How could they maintain their beliefs and culture far from their beloved land? The answer lay in their stories, prayers, and traditions, which they carried in their hearts like precious treasures.

The legends of the Kingdom of Israel are not just stories of the past; they are reflections of human experiences that resonate even today. They invite us to ponder profound questions: What does it mean to believe in something greater than ourselves?

How do we find hope in times of despair? And what role do our stories play in shaping who we are?

As we conclude this chapter filled with mysteries and myths, let us remember that the ancient Kingdom of Israel is a reminder of the power of storytelling. Each tale holds lessons that can guide us through our own lives, just as they guided the people of Israel through theirs.

Key Takeaway: Stories have the power to inspire and teach us valuable lessons, connecting us to our past and helping us navigate our future.

Dear Cool Kids/Parents

Thank you for choosing "What the History"! We hope this book has ignited a spark of wonder and motivation within you.

If you found this book captivating and believe in the transformative power of its message, we kindly ask for your support. Please consider leaving a glowing review on the platform where you purchased the book. Your review will help spread this message of empowerment to even more young readers, inspiring them to dream big and reach for the stars.

The core essence of this book - to inspire and uplift young minds - is what truly matters. We acknowledge that perfection is elusive, and we appreciate your understanding and forgiveness for any minor imperfections.

Thank you for being a part of our mission to nurture the brilliance and potential within the next generation. Your feedback will go a long way in helping us continue to provide captivating and transformative stories for young readers.

The Kingdom of Israel

Made in United States
North Haven, CT
27 May 2025